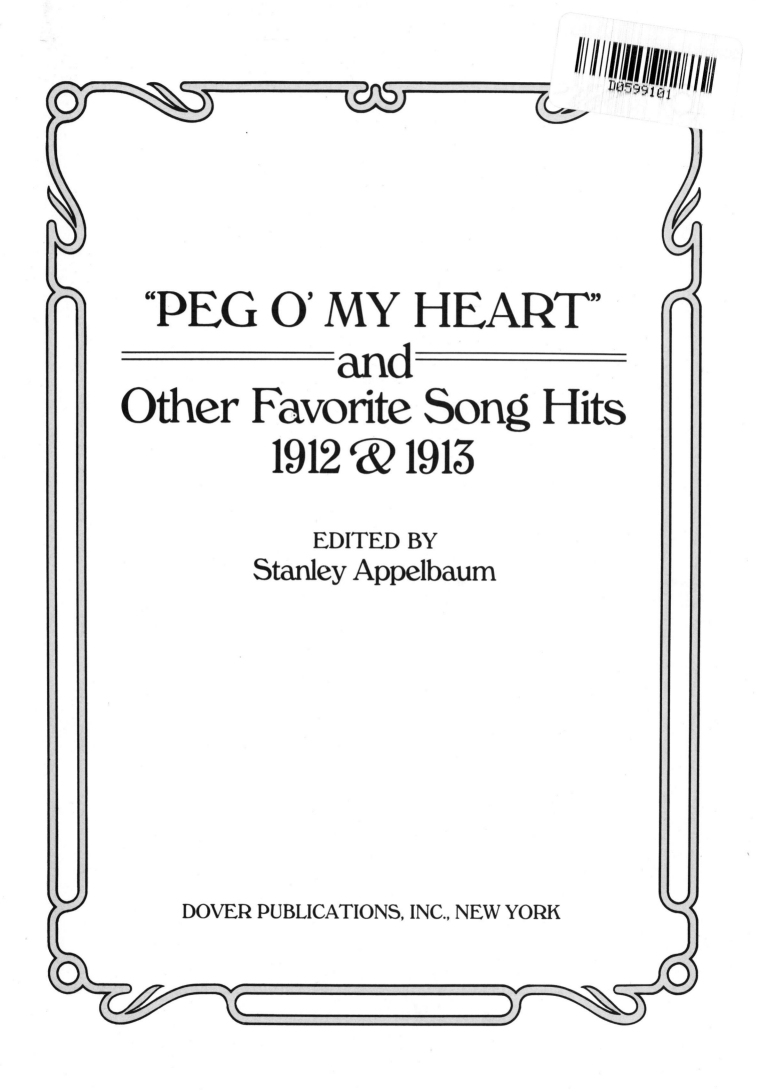

"PEG O' MY HEART"

and

Other Favorite Song Hits
1912 & 1913

EDITED BY
Stanley Appelbaum

DOVER PUBLICATIONS, INC., NEW YORK

ACKNOWLEDGMENTS

The publisher and editor are grateful to Sandy Marrone for lending the original sheet music of "The Old Rugged Cross" and "The Sweetheart of Sigma Chi," and to David A. Jasen for lending "Peg o' My Heart."

All the other music was loaned by the ARCHIVE OF POPULAR AMERICAN MUSIC, UCLA. The publisher and editor particularly wish to thank the Archive and its Head, Victor T. Cardell, for the splendid cooperation that made this volume possible.

Published in Canada by General Publishing Company, Ltd.,
30 Lesmill Road, Don Mills, Toronto, Ontario.
Published in the United Kingdom by Constable and Company, Ltd.,
10 Orange Street, London WC2H 7EG.

"Peg o' My Heart" and Other Favorite Song Hits, 1912 & 1913 is a new work, first published by Dover Publications, Inc., in 1989. It consists of unabridged, unaltered republications of the sheet music of 36 popular songs (original publishers and dates of publication are indicated in the Contents) and a new Introduction.

Manufactured in the United States of America
Dover Publications, Inc.
31 East 2nd Street
Mineola, N.Y. 11501

Library of Congress Cataloging-in-Publication Data

"Peg o' my heart" and other favorite song hits, 1912 & 1913.

For voice and piano.
Reproduces the original sheet music of 36 popular songs.
1. Popular music—1911–1920. I. Appelbaum, Stanley.
II. Title: Peg o' my heart.
M1630.18.P43   1989   88-754538
ISBN 0-486-25998-6

INTRODUCTION

The number of hit songs from 1912 and 1913 that are still fondly remembered and sung today is almost astonishing when compared with the harvest of even the very rich preceding years. The present anthology, which reproduces original or early publications of 36 of these songs, is a wide-ranging one that caters to many tastes and includes just about every popular genre of the time. Most of the pieces naturally represent continuations of trends already current, particularly ragtime, but there are also foretastes of new things to come, and even in such traditional areas as the operetta there are exciting new debuts.

Roughly a third of the contents can be considered as ragtime, which was clearly the leading genre of that period, and clearly at a peak in 1912 and 1913 with such new entries as "Waiting for the Robert E. Lee" and "Ballin' the Jack." (The latter is also an outstanding early example of dance instructions being imparted, however sketchily, in the lyric itself.) Nor was there any exaggeration in Irving Berlin's claim, in "That International Rag," that the genre was rapidly conquering Europe as well.

The ragtime song of this era was not such a tightly controlled composition as the classic piano rag, but was characterized by simple though effective syncopations, and more particularly by brief repeated catchphrases (musical and verbal), such as "Hitchy Koo" (in the song of that name), "Poogy-woo" (in "Snookey Ookums") and countless others. These repeated phrases were no doubt integral to the various animal-inspired dances (grizzly bear, bunny hug, turkey trot, etc.) that were performed to the music and some of whose features are enshrined in many a lyric: shoulder-heaving, finger-snapping and cries of "It's a bear!" (meaning "It's great" or "It's top-notch"). The grand perennial "You Made Me Love You" seems to have this phrase repetition as its basic structural principle— "I didn't want to do it," "Yes I do, Deed I do, You know I do," "Give me give me what I [cry for]"—but is no less of a well-rounded whole for all that.

The tremendous energy and vitality of this simplified ragtime made it a perfect medium for songs about locomotion. Within this subgenre, private transportation especially is often associated with lovemaking. "In My Merry Oldsmobile" of 1905 had pointed the way with its phrase "You can go as far as you like with me."

"He'd Have to Get Under" of 1913 is one big double entendre, in which the frustrated hero, at his moments of ardor, is constantly let down by "his little machine." Likewise, in "Row, Row, Row" of 1912, there is little doubt that Johnnie's frenetic rowing throughout the song is a stand-in for another kinetic activity.

Train travel is usually for other purposes. In 1912 Irving Berlin produced one of the great train songs, "When the Midnight Choo-Choo Leaves for Alabam'," which is also a classic statement of the going-home and going-South themes that were already very popular and were destined to become even more so. Of course, Berlin was the preeminent songwriter of these years and was full or part creator of five of the ragtime and novelty numbers in this volume. In 1912, however, he also wrote the autobiographical "When I Lost You," the first of his more lyrical pieces to win over the public, which would eventually associate him primarily with this more sentimental type of composition (the "Berlin ballad").

Other imperishable ballads of 1912 and 1913 included here are "Moonlight Bay" (by Percy Wenrich, also noted for "Put On Your Old Grey Bonnet" of 1909 and a number of minor-classic piano rags), "My Melancholy Baby," "If I Had My Way" and "The Sweetheart of Sigma Chi"—the last three, surprisingly, all by "one-shot" songwriters outside of the Tin Pan Alley mainstream.

The rich field of Irish-American songs is represented by one of its greatest hits, "When Irish Eyes Are Smiling," by Ernest R. Ball, who had already given us "Mother Machree" in 1910.

One odd throwback in 1913 was "The Curse of an Aching Heart," in which everything—situation, sentiment, lyric and tune—were right out of the early nineties!

Two songs of 1912 and 1913, one a typical English spoof-the-Irish novelty item, the other a sort of dreamy march (written by Americans but published in London), were not particularly successful until their adoption by British troops in the First World War immortalized them: "It's a Long, Long Way to Tipperary" and "There's a Long, Long Trail."

In the world of operetta, the old master Victor Herbert had a well-deserved success with *Sweethearts* in 1913. The title waltz song, more in the dashing Lehár vein than many of its Herbert predecessors, is one of the finest of its type ever composed in America. But two new writers of operetta were about to make their mark here.

The Firefly of 1912, Rudolf Friml's first popular success, was an act of rivalry with Herbert in more ways than one. The star was Emma Trentini, who had been Herbert's (naughty) Marietta two years earlier but now hired Friml, instead, to write her new vehicle. And—as the cover of "Giannina Mia" reveals—that number was billed as an "Italian Street Song"! (The "Giannina Mia" sheet music also shows that the "Gian-" was intended to be pronounced correctly as a *single* syllable.) The opening of another number, "Love Is Like a Firefly," is remarkably reminiscent of the opening of Paul Lincke's "The Glow-Worm" (1902, introduced to the U.S. in 1907).

The other new master of operetta, Emmerich (Imre) Kálmán, was already established in Vienna, but *Sári* was his first American triumph. Of its numbers, "Love's Own Sweet Song" (or at least its waltz music) seems to have held up best over the years.

So much for the ongoing genres and traditions as reflected in 1912 and 1913. Among the new trends that manifested themselves in those two years, probably the most important was the commercial exploitation of the blues. No less a figure than W. C. Handy wrote the music of "The Memphis Blues," which in its song version of 1913 transferred this major American genre from Southern farms and ghettos to the glitter of big-city show business.

Also about this time, the Euro-American hymn was becoming an entertainment item of sorts. Homer Rodeheaver, for twenty years a choir leader, vocalist and trombonist for the itinerant revivalist Billy Sunday, soon founded publishing and recording companies of his own, and a number of standard gospel pieces, some devotional and some more upbeat, were first printed by him. One of the most enduring has been "The Old Rugged Cross."

Latin-American rhythms had been heard intermittently in U.S. popular music, but their real popularity, which continues unabated today, was another consequence of the dance craze of the early 1910s. The tango, probably based on Cuban antecedents, was nurtured in the slums of Buenos Aires and then sanitized in Parisian ballrooms before reaching our shores. "El Choclo" was the first international tango standard, so important historically that it had to be included here even though it is an instrumental and not strictly a song.

Mexico, on the other hand, was not adequately represented by Victor Schertzinger's "Marchéta (A Love Song of Old Mexico)," a quiet waltz with no distinctive Latin flavor. Some years were still to pass before such real Mexican songs as "La Cucaracha" and "Cielito Lindo" came and conquered. "Marchéta" made a reputation for Schertzinger, but his scores for such films as *The Love Parade* (1929) and *The Fleet's In* (1942) were to prove much more full-blooded.

A great deal could be added about the careers of the songwriters, lyricists and publishers included in the present volume, but it seemed preferable to leave more space for the music itself and merely to indicate trends in this Introduction. But even a quick reading of the credits in the table of contents that follows will reveal how busy some of the Tin Pan Alley professionals could be in only two years of activity.

Reluctantly, not much more will be said here about the great entertainers who brought these songs before the public. It would be almost criminal, however, to omit the briefest mention of the phenomenal popularity enjoyed even at this early date by Al Jolson, who could make a hit of just about any song that he could be prevailed upon to "introduce" at his appearances. "Waiting for the Robert E. Lee" and "You Made Me Love You" in this volume are two of the numbers for which he did the honors.

Finally, a few explanatory notes. Two of the songs included here were inspired by, and used the names of, stage successes of the period: "Jimmy Valentine" (about a genial housebreaker) and "Peg o' My Heart" (see the cover of the latter song, which features a photograph of Laurette Taylor in the title role); while another song, "The Trail of the Lonesome Pine," refers to a popular novel. The "Jimmy Valentine" cover shows part of the membership (at the moment) of Gus Edwards' famous vaudeville act, in which he appeared alongside talented child protégés (Eddie Cantor, Walter Winchell and George Jessel were just three of the alumni of this professional "school"). The Eva Tanguay mentioned in one of the additional verses of "My Wife's Gone to the Country" was a top vaudeville headliner, and "I Don't Care," which she introduced in 1905, was her rackety, libertarian theme song. The Italian musical direction at the beginning of "Marchéta" should read "Come un *sogno.*"

CONTENTS

The songs are arranged in alphabetical order, using their titles as printed either on the first page of music of the original sheets or else on the cover, and not counting "A" or "The" at the beginning of the title. The publishers given here (abbreviated "Pub.") are those indicated on the covers of the specific first or early editions being reprinted. The years given are those of copyright.

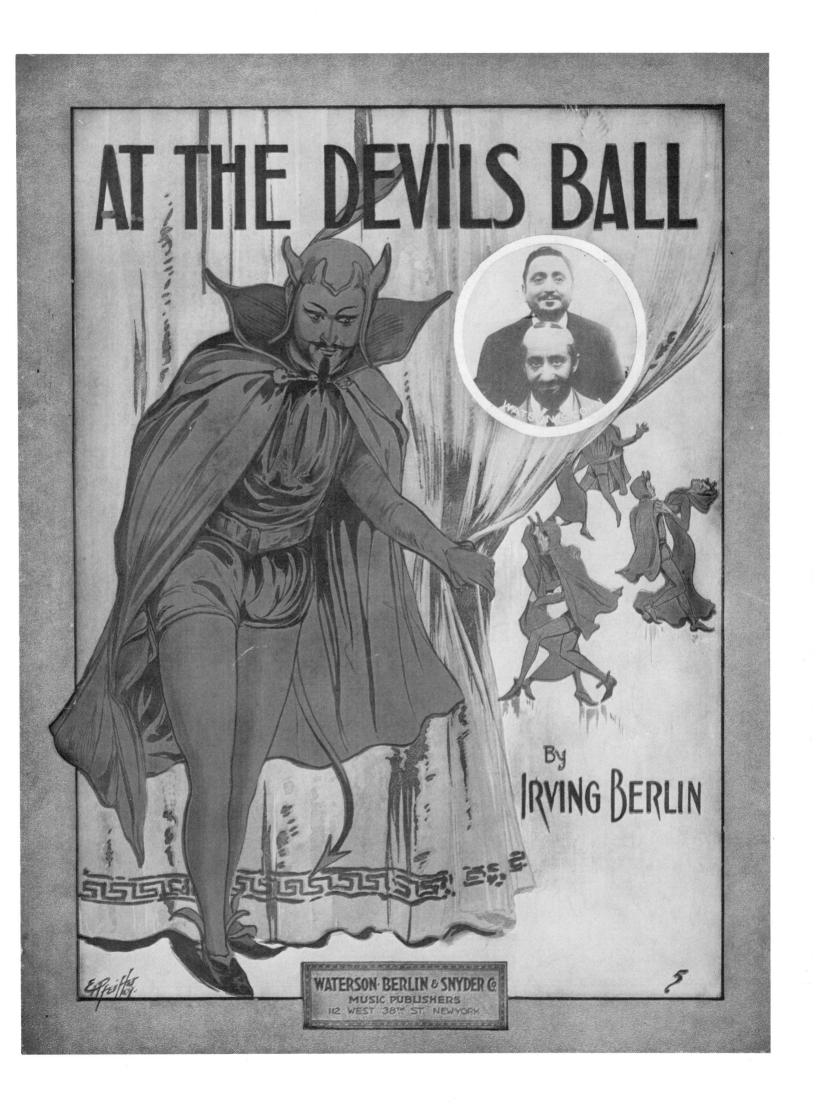

AT THE DEVIL'S BALL.

By IRVING BERLIN.

Devil's Ball,_____ In the Devil's Hall,_____ I saw the

funniest dev - il that I ever saw Taking the tickets from folks at the door;

I caught a glimpse of my mother - in - law Dancing with the Dev-il,

Oh! the lit-tle Devil, Dancing at the Devil's Ball._____ At the Ball._____

D.S.

Ballin' The Jack

Words by
JIM BURRIS

Music by
CHRIS SMITH

Folks in Geor - gia's
It's being done at

'bout to go in-sane   Since that new dance   down in Georgia came,
all the Ca-bar- ets,   All so-cie-ty   now has got the craze,

I'm the on-ly per-son who's to blame I'm the par-ty in-tro-duced it
It's the best dance done in mo-dern days That is why I rave a-bout it

there, so! Give me cre-dit to know a thing or two Give me cre-dit
so, Play some good Rag, that will make you prance Old folks,young folks

for spring-ing something new I will show this lit-tle dance to you
all try to do the dance, Join right in now while you got the chance

When I do you'll say that it's a bear.
Once a-gain the steps to you I'll show.

Be My Little Baby Bumble Bee

Words by
STANLEY MURPHY

Music by
HENRY I. MARSHALL

12

Bil - ly Bum - ble used to mum - ble Round the Rose ma -
Pa - pa bee said Good - ness me!" And ma - ma said "We'll

ry, Where she would meet him greet him and then treat him
see If you can pay your way, for ev - ry day the

To some hon - ey sprees, Then start a - buz - zin'
price of hon - ey grows dear?" But lit - tle queen-ie said:

in a doz - en diff - 'rent lov - in' keys.
"That for Swee-ney," and whis - pered in his ear:

The Curse Of An Aching Heart.

Words by
HENRY FINK.

Music by
AL. PIANTADOSI.

You made me think you cared for me, And I be-
The dreams I dreamed of fut - ure joys You smiled on,

lieved in you,_____ You told me things you ne - er meant, And
though you knew,_____ Deep down with - in your faitht - less heart, They

made me think them true._____ I gam-bled in the game of
nev - er would come true,_____ Still fur-ther on you lead me

love, I played my heart and lost,_____ I'm now a
till My par - a - dise I saw,_____ Then with one

wreck, Up - on life's sea, A - lone I pay the cost._____
word you ban - ished all my hopes for ev - er-more._____

CHORUS.

You made me what I am to-day, I hope you're sat - is -

 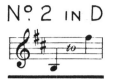 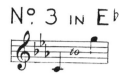 

Nº 1 in C   Nº 2 in D   Nº 3 in E♭   Nº 4 in F

SUNG BY
MME. SCHUMANN-HEINK, MISS FLORENCE HINKLE
AND
MR. DAN BEDDOE

DANNY BOY

✴ Song ✴

ADAPTED FROM AN

Old Irish Air

BY

FRED. E. WEATHERLY

Ⓐ

Boosey & Company, Inc.

NEW YORK: STEINWAY HALL, 113 WEST 57TH ST.
LONDON, ENG.: BOOSEY & CO., LTD., 295 REGENT ST., W.I.

DANNY BOY.

Words by
FRED. E. WEATHERLY.

Adapted from
an Old Irish Air by
FRED. E. WEATHERLY.

Oh, Dan-ny Boy the pipes, the pipes are call-ing ___ From glen to glen, and down the moun-tain side, _____ The sum-mer's

hear, though soft you tread a - bove me,____ And all my

grave will warm - er, sweet - er be,____ For you will

bend and tell me that you love_ me,____ And I shall

sleep in peace un - til you come to me!_____

EL CHOCLO

TANGO ARGENTINO

BY

A. G. VILLOLDO

With an Introduction on the Theory of the real
Tango Argentino and a Description of the Dance

BY PROF. L. ROBERT OF PARIS

Price 50c

NEW YORK : G. SCHIRMER · BOSTON : THE BOSTON MUSIC CO.

DIRECTIONS FOR DANCING
THE REAL TANGO ARGENTINO

by

L. ROBERT

Director of the

Académie de Danse Mondaine, Paris

The Tango, of South American origin, is danced in very slow time, somewhat in the style of the habanera. The following steps have been fitted and adapted to *El Choclo*, by A. G. Villoldo, one of the few genuine Tangos as they are danced in South America.

DESCRIPTION OF THE DANCE

I.   The gentleman, holding the lady (who faces him) somewhat to his right and outside his right foot, backs her at a measured and graceful walk for about half a dozen steps; he then executes the following step:

Step forward on right foot, slide left foot to the left (toe pointing out), draw right foot alongside the left, then step with it to the rear, bending the knee simultaneously. (The lady executes this step starting backward with her left foot and at the finish with her right foot well forward.)

II.   The gentleman starts off to the rear, the lady forward:

Cross the right foot behind the left, then the left before the right—left heel slightly raised and out, left toe slightly in. Then step back with left, leaving right in place pointing toe out, and slightly bend left knee.

III.   The gentleman starts forward, the lady to the rear:

Cross left foot before and over right, place right foot to the right, heel slightly raised and out, then step forward on right, bend right knee, slightly raising left heel.

N. B.   When the gentleman goes to the rear, the lady executes step III.

When the gentleman goes forward, the lady executes step II.

IV.   The lady and gentleman dance a waltz-step to the left one or more times, and repeat step II or III.

V.   (The Figure Eight.)

The gentleman crosses the right foot before the left, draws the left around and next to the right, steps back with the right;—then crosses the left foot before the right, draws the right around and next to the left, steps forward with the left.

This is repeated several times.

(The lady does the same.)

VI.   A few steps to the side, cross right foot before left, point left toe out, then left crosses before right, point right toe out.

VII.   Both execute walk which connects each individual step. Each makes a turn, the gentleman passing in front of the lady and the lady passing in front of the gentleman.

VIII.   Both take a few sliding steps to one side; the gentleman raises himself on his toes, turning slowly in position while the lady circles around him with a gliding step.

IX.   (The Square.)

The gentleman steps forward with right, slides left to the left, draws right next to left, steps back with left, draws right alongside left. Similarly on starting with left foot.

L. ROBERT.

26

El Choclo

Tango Argentino

A. G. Villoldo
Arranged and edited by
G. J. S. W.

27

THE FIREFLY
A Comedy-Opera

BY

OTTO HAUERBACH & RUDOLF FRIML

PRODUCED UNDER THE MANAGEMENT OF MR. ARTHUR HAMMERSTEIN

VOCAL SCORE 2.00 *net*   SELECTIONS FROM THE OPERA 1.00 *net*

PUBLISHED SEPARATELY

FOR VOICE AND PIANO

Love is like a Firefly. (Nina) High in F, Low in D

Something. (Jenkins and Suzette) Duet for Soprano and Tenor

Giannina mia. (*Italian Street Song.*) (Nina) High in E, Low in C

In Sapphire Seas. (*Barcarolle.*) (Sybil) High

Tommy Atkins. (Nina and ensemble) High

Sympathy. (*Waltz-Song.*) (Geraldine and Thurston) Medium

A Woman's Smile. (Jack) High in F, Low in D

The Beautiful Ship from Toyland. (Franz) Bass

When a maid comes knocking at your heart. (Nina) High in F, Low in D

The Dawn of Love. (L'Alba d'amore) (*Concert waltz, English and Italian.*) (Nina) High in F, Low in E♭

Pr. 60c each

FOR PIANO SOLO

The Firefly Waltzes   Pr. 75c

The Firefly March and Two-Step   Pr. 60c

CHORUSES WITH PIANO ACCOMPANIMENT

No. 5711. In Sapphire Seas. (Sybil and Mixed Chorus)   net 12c

No. 5710. The Beautiful Ship from Toyland. (Franz and Men's Chorus)   net 25c

NEW YORK : G. SCHIRMER

BOSTON : THE BOSTON MUSIC CO.

Giannina mia

Nina

Words by
Otto Hauerbach

From the Comedy-Opera
"The Firefly," by
Rudolf Friml

sleeps the dream - ing moon._____ I'll___ fash - ion a
night's ob - lit - -'ring shade._____ And the pearls that I

crown you'll a - dore _____ From the gold that lies shim-mer - ing
place in your hair _____ Will die as the gold and its

there,_____ And the sil - ver-y pearls from the drip-ping oar_____
sheen;_____ You a - lone will re - main for me ra-diant there,_____

I will set in your hair._____
You shall still be my queen._____

1.-2. For____ I a - dore,____ I a-dore you, Gian-ni-na mi - a! More,____ more and

more,____ I a - dore you, Gian-ni-na mi - a! Queens there have been, who in

ag - es of old Shone more re-splendent with jew - els and gold,

Pre-cious jew-els not half so rare, dear,____ As the splen-dor____

He'd Have To Get Under – Get Out And Get Under
(TO FIX UP HIS AUTOMOBILE)

Words by
GRANT CLARKE and
EDGAR LESLIE

Music by
MAURICE ABRAHAMS

Allegretto

Till ready

John-ny O' Con - nor bought an au-to-mo - bile, __ He took his sweet-heart for a
Mill-ion-aire Wil - son said to John-ny one day, __ Your lit-tle sweet-heart don't ap-

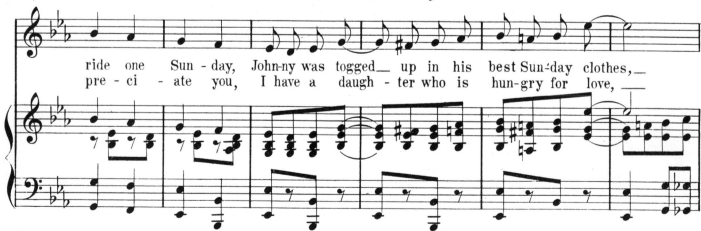

ride one Sun - day, John-ny was togged __ up in his best Sun-day clothes, __
pre - ci - ate you, I have a daugh - ter who is hun-gry for love, __

CHORUS

have to get un - der, get out and get un - der To fix his

lit - tle ma - chine, _____ He was just dy - ing to

cud - dle his queen, _ But ev'-ry min -ute when he'd be -

gin it, He'd have to get un - der, get out and get un - der,

Then he'd get back at the wheel _____ A doz-en times they'd

start to hug and kiss_ And then the darned old en - gine it would miss_

_ And then he'd have to get un - der, get out and get un - der, And

fix up his au - to-mo - bile. _____ He'd bile. _____

"Hitchy Koo."

Words by
L. WOLFE GILBERT.

Music by
LEWIS F. MUIR &
MAURICE ABRAHAMS.

If you've got an ear for mu-sic then just
Oh it acts just like a ton-ic to my

gath - er near, ___ Tell me, can't you hear it buz - zin'
love - sick heart, ___ I can - not wait till eve - ning till that

in your ear;___ Is it mu - sic? sure it's mu - sic, it's the
thing will start;___ Do I love it? sure I love it, of my

best you'll ev - er hear, It's my ev - er lov-in' hon-ey, call - ing
life it is a part, like the voice of cu - pid send - ing me his

ba - by dear,_____ Say ain't that mu - sic weired,
lit - tle dart._____ Say ain't that mu - sic weired,

strang-est you ev - er heered? Say, don't you be___ a-skeered lis - ten!
strang-est you ev - er heered? Say, don't you be___ a-skeered lis - ten!

CHORUS.

Oh._____ ev - ry evening hear him sing,_____ it's the cut-est lit-tle

thing,_____ got the cutest lit-tle swing, Hitchy Koo, Hitchy Koo, Hitchy Koo.

Oh_____ simply meant for Kings and queens._____ don't you ask me what it

means,_____ I just love that Hit-chy Koo, Hit-chy Koo, Hit-chy

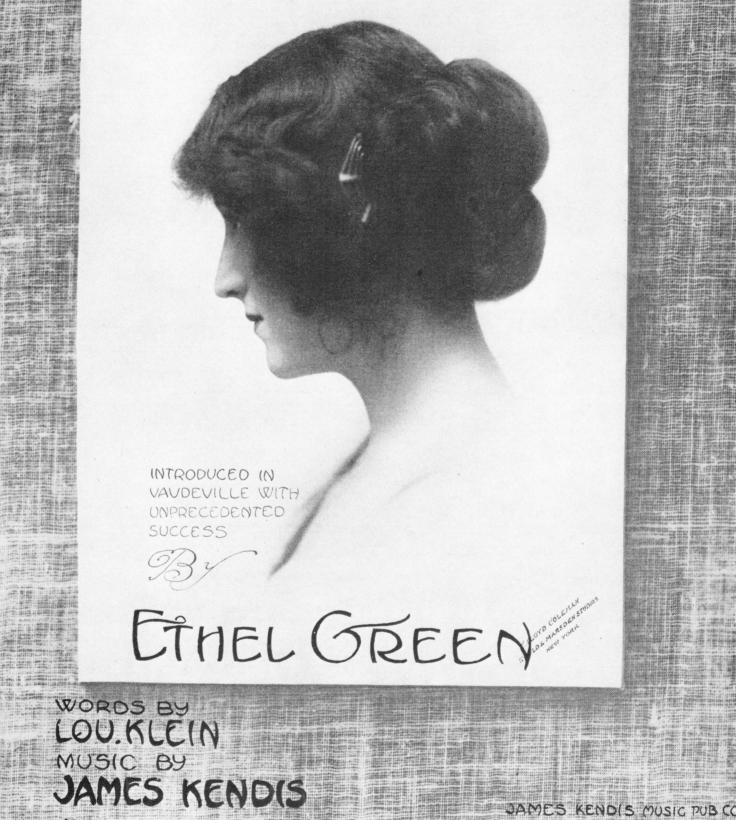

If I Had My Way.

(BALLAD)

Words by
LOU KLEIN.

Music by
JAMES KENDIS.

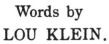

I'd like to make your gold - en dreams come
You'd nev - er know a care, a pain, or

true, dear,   If I on - ly had my way,_____   A
sor - row,   If I on - ly had my way,_____   I'd

par - a - dise this world would seem to you, dear,　　If
fill your cup of hap - pi - ness to - mor - row,　　If

I on - ly had my way. _____
I on - ly had my way. _____

CHORUS.
Valse lento. *Not too fast*

If I had my way, dear, for - ev - er there'd be a gar - den of

ros - es for you and for me, A thou - sand and one things,dear, I would

THE SONG THEY SING AS THEY MARCH ALONG

IT'S A LONG, LONG WAY TO TIPPERARY

WRITTEN AND COMPOSED BY

JACK JUDGE

AND

HARRY WILLIAMS

Price 50 Cents Net

Except Canada and Foreign Countries

CHAPPELL & CO., LTD.

MELBOURNE LONDON SYDNEY

FOR THE COUNTRIES OF NORTH AMERICA

CHAPPELL & CO · INC · RKO BUILDING ROCKEFELLER CENTER · N · Y · C

"It's a long, long way to Tipperary."

BAND PARTS READY 1/-

Written & Composed by

JACK JUDGE & HARRY WILLIAMS.

Allegro con Spirito.

Up to migh-ty Lon-don came an Ir-ish-man one day,
Pad-dy wrote a let-ter to his Ir-ish Mol-ly O',
Mol-ly wrote a neat re-ply to Ir-ish Pad-dy O',

London: B. FELDMAN & Cᵒ, 2 & 3, Arthur Street, New Oxford Street, W. C.

FOR THE UNITED STATES OF AMERICA: CHAPPELL & CO., LTD.

RKO BUILDING - ROCKEFELLER CENTER   NEW YORK, N.Y.

As the streets are paved with gold, sure ev-'ry-one was gay;
Say-ing,"Should you not re-ceive it, write and let me know!
Say-ing,"Mike Ma - lon-ey wants to mar-ry me, and so

Sing-ing songs of Pic-ca-dil-ly, Strand and Leices-ter Square, Till
"If I make mis - takes in "spell-ing," Mol-ly dear," said he, "Re-
Leave the Strand and Pic - ca-dil-ly, or you'll be to blame, For

Pad-dy got ex - cit-ed, then he shout-ed to them there:—
-mem-ber it's the pen that's bad, don't lay the blame on me"
love has fair-ly drove me sil-ly— hop-ing you're the same!"

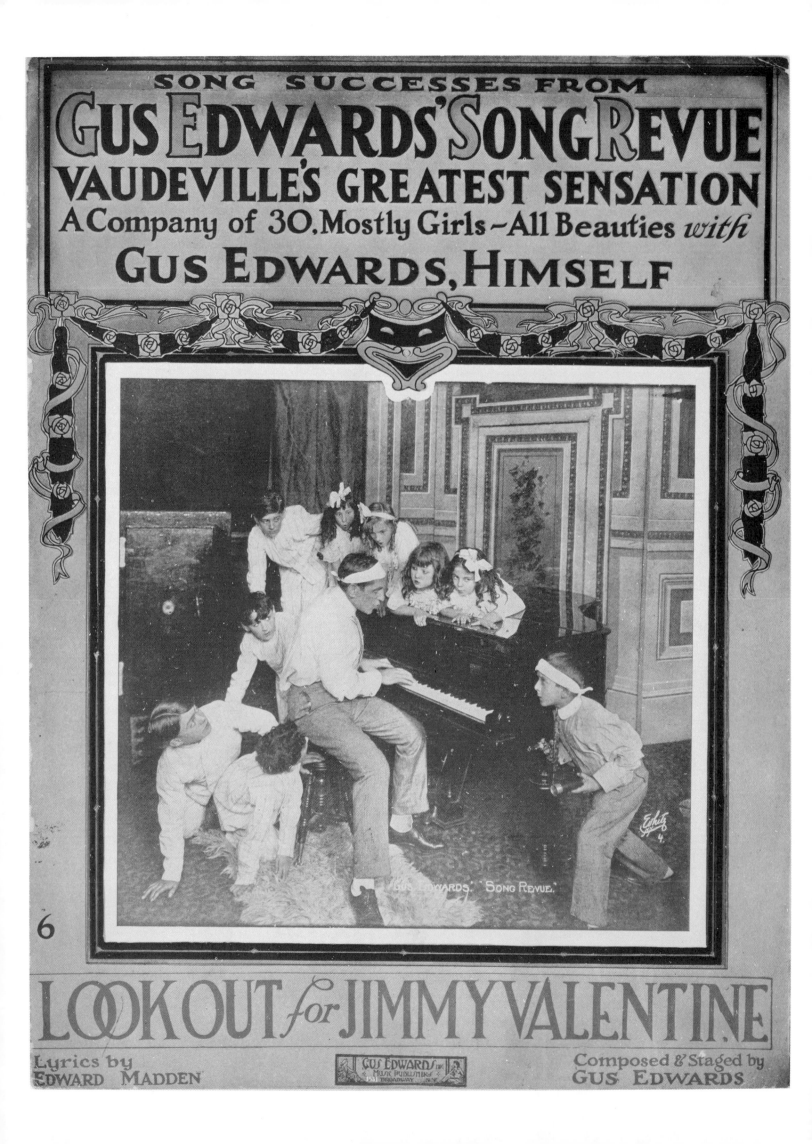

Jimmy Valentine.

Words by
EDWARD MADDEN.

Music by
GUS EDWARDS.

When the stars a - bove are
Through a mask two eyes gleam

blink - ing   And the house is dark and still_____ And a
bright - ly   As they rove in search of loot,_____ While a

Look out, look out, look out for Jim- mie Va- len -tine

For he's a pal of mine A sen - ti- men- tal crook With a

touch that lin- gers In his sand - -pap -ered fin -gers He can

find the com - bi - na - tion of your pock - et - book Look

out,   look out,   for   when you see   his lan - tern shine

That's   the time   to   jump right   up   and   shout   Help!   He'd

steal   a horse and cart   He'd ev - en   steal   a girl - ie's heart When Jim - my

Va - len-tine   gets · out.   Look   out.

Love Is Like a Firefly

Nina

Words by
Otto Hauerbach

From the Comedy-Opera
"The Firefly," by
Rudolf Friml

INTRODUCTION
Moderato

Piano

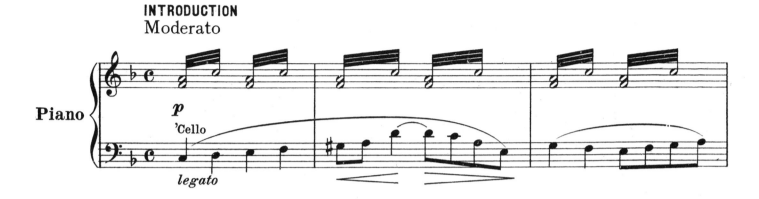

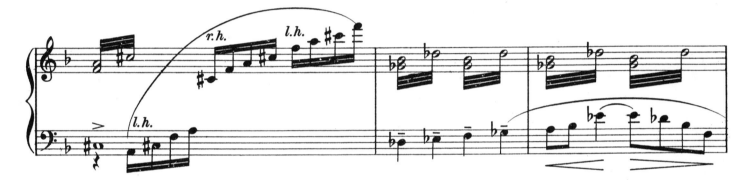

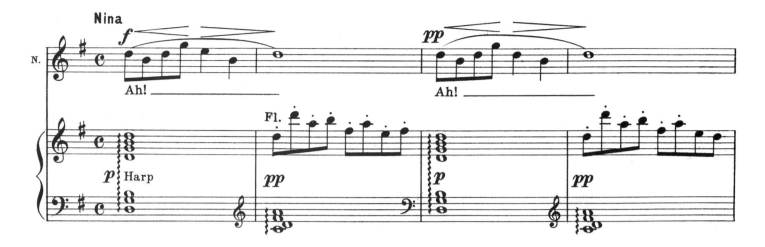

1. La-dies fair, la-dies fair, Hear me! I've some-thing new to tell to you.
2. La-dies fair, If you care Dear - ly De-light-ful wedding-steps to take,

If I please, if I please, Cheer me! But don't for - get your pen - nies,
An - gle not, Dan - gle not; Clear - ly, The stout-est strings are known to

too. La - dies fair, la - dies fair, Heed me! I'm
break. Gen - tle - men, Be you then War - - y!

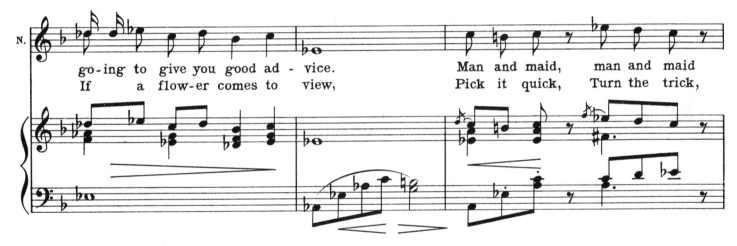

go - ing to give you good ad - vice. Man and maid, man and maid
If a flow - er comes to view, Pick it quick, Turn the trick,

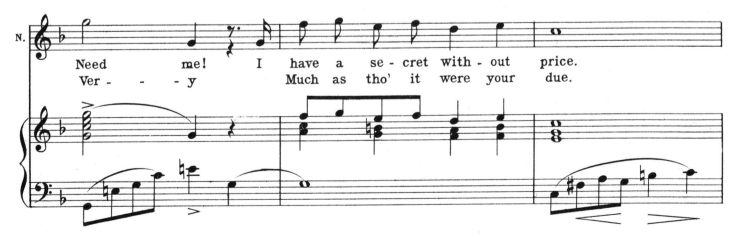

Need me! I have a se - cret with - out price.
Ver - - y Much as tho' it were your due.

Love Is Like a Firefly   61

Maid - ens who with love - thoughts burn,
There - fore do not hes - i - tate,

Lads who for sweet la - dies yearn,
Do not make a maid - en wait;

Hear me! Come gath - er
Snatch her, If you would

near me: This sim - ple les - son you all should learn:
catch her! Or you will find it is all too late.

Quasi gavotta

1-2. Love is like a fire - fly That glimmers by, And dies while it is gleam - ing.

There-fore when you see it nigh,___ You must be ver-y spry, Ev-er sly,

Nev-er shy. When with-in her twink-ling eye___ You see the

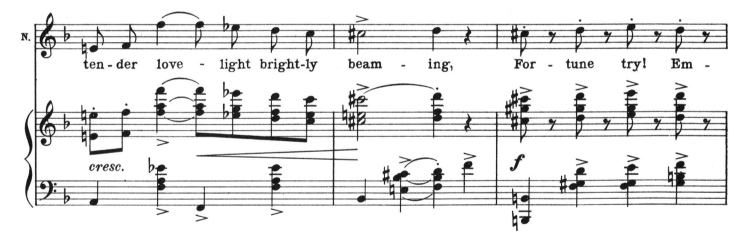

ten-der love-light bright-ly beam - ing, For-tune try! Em -

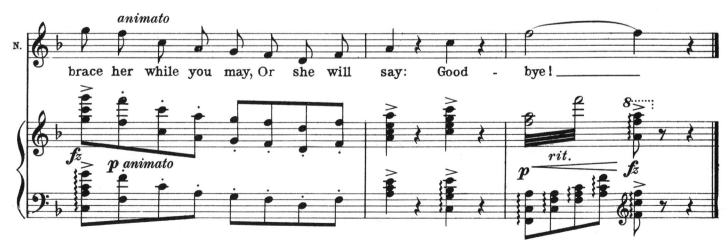

brace her while you may, Or she will say: Good - bye!_____

LOVE'S OWN SWEET SONG

HENRY W. SAVAGE'S
NEW OPERETTE

SÁRI
(DER ZIGEUNERPRIMAS)

BOOK BY

JULIUS WILHELM

&

FRITZ GRÜNBAUM

ENGLISH ADAPTATION BY

C. C. S. CUSHING

&

E. P. HEATH

VOCAL

MUSIC BY

EMMERICH KÁLMÁN

Published by JOS. W. STERN & CO.

JOSEF WEINBERGER - LEIPZIG

Love's Own Sweet Song

Lyric by
C. C. S. CUSHING
& E. P. HEATH.

Music by
EMMERICH KÁLMÁN.

Tempo di Valse

In the toils of love I'm caught,___ Hap - pi - ness I
Love to us has lent his wings,___ To the waltz what

have been taught,___ I knew not the bliss, Of a lov-er's kiss;
joys he brings,___ Here and there we go, Glid-ing to and fro,

I had nev-er dreamed there was a joy like this. Dear one I feel
Like a bit of this-tle-down when breez-es blow, Al-ways shall we

just the same,___ With-out you my life is tame,___
dance like this,___ Al-ways shall we know such bliss,___

All I want is you, No one else will do, Love and love a-
Down through life I'll glide, Ev-er at your side, You shall be my

REFRAIN

lone is all to blame.___
bride what ere be-tide.___ Oh let us come and dance with joy Since

love and life are ours,_____ For youth is strong and blood grows

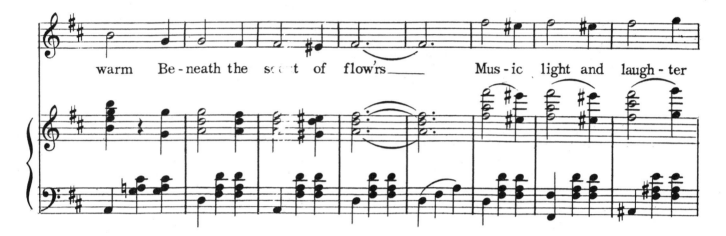

warm Be-neath the scent of flow'rs_____ Mus-ic light and laugh-ter

bright shall car-ry us a-long_____ Sing-ing with our

hearts on fire love's own sweet song._____ song._____

MARCHÉTA

(A Love Song of Old Mexico)

POEM
AND
MUSIC
BY

Victor Schertzinger.

— 6 —

Publishers,

The John Franklin Music Co.
1531 BROADWAY,
NEW YORK.

MARCHĒTA

Poem & Music
VICTOR L. SCHERTZINGER.

Come un Sonnio.

Dreamily.

Mar - che - ta, Mar - che - ta, I still hear you call - ing me back to your arms once a -

gain,_____ I still feel the spell of your last kiss up-

on me, Since then, life, has all been in vain._____

All has been sad-ness with-out you Mar-che-ta, Each

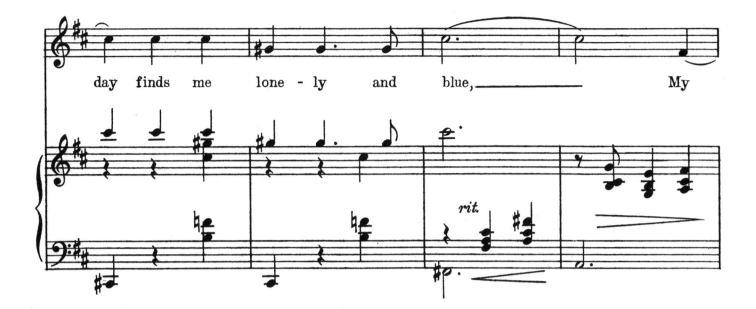

day finds me lone - ly and blue,_____ My

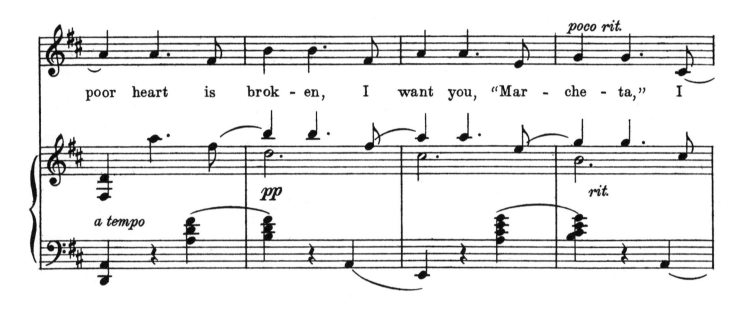

poor heart is brok - en, I want you, "Mar - che - ta," I

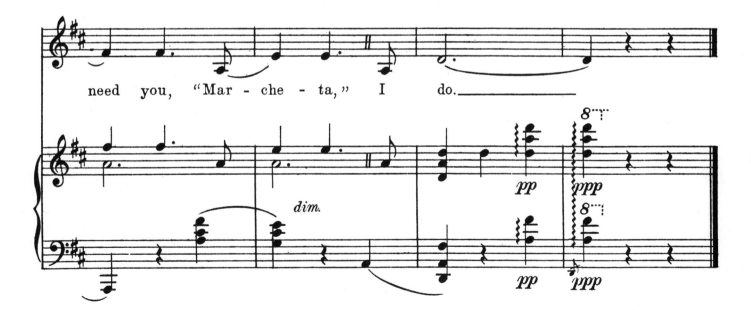

need you, "Mar - che - ta," I do._____

THE MEMPHIS BLUES

SUCCESSFULLY
FEATURED BY
ED. V. CUPERO'S
BAND AND ORCHESTRA

IN
GEO. EVANS'
"HONEY BOY"
MINSTRELS

GEO. EVANS'
HONEY BOY
MINSTRELS

ED. V. CUPERO
Musical Director
HONEY BOY "EVANS MINSTREL'S

A SOUTHERN
RAG
BY
W. C. HANDY

GEO. A. NORTON'S
SONG
FOUNDED ON W.C. HANDY'S
WORLD WIDE "BLUE" MELODY

T. J. JOHNSTON
PIANO AND MUSIC HOUSE
VICTOR AND COLUMBIA
TALKING MACHINES
MAIN STREET 415 S. MAIN ST. HOME A-5738
LOS ANGELES CALIFORNIA

JOE MORRIS MUSIC CO.
Sole Selling Agents
145 West 45th Street
New York.

THE MEMPHIS BLUES.

GEORGE A. NORTON'S..
Song
Founded on W. C. Handy's World Wide "Blue" Note Melody.

Folks I've just been down, down to Mem-phis town, That's where the peo - ple smile,
Oh, that mel - o - dy, sure ap - pealed to me, Just like a moun-tain stream

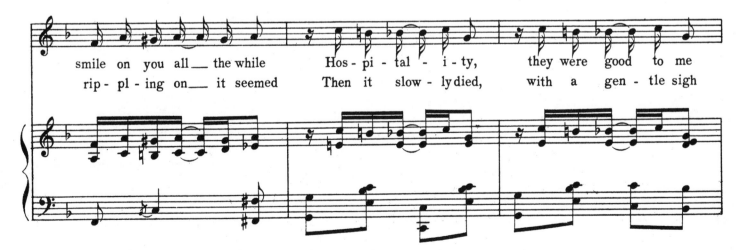

smile on you all __ the while Hos - pi - tal - i - ty, they were good to me
rip - pl - ing on __ it seemed Then it slow - ly died, with a gen - tle sigh

Day, on Re - viv - al Day, _____ That mel - an - cho - ly strain that e - ver

haunt-ing re - frain is like a Dark - ies sor - row song _____ Here comes the

ver - y part that wraps a spell a - round my heart, _____

heart, _____ It sets me wild to hear that lov - in' tune a -

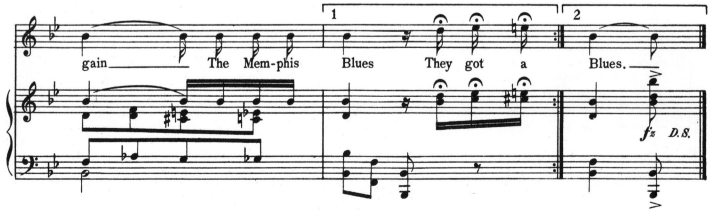

gain _____ The Mem-phis Blues They got a Blues. _____

POPULAR EDITION
MOONLIGHT BAY
SONG
WORDS BY
EDWARD MADDEN
MUSIC BY
PERCY WENRICH
5
JEROME H. REMICK & CO
NEW YORK DETROIT

Moonlight Bay

Words by
EDWARD MADDEN

Music by
PERCY WENRICH

Voic - es   hum, croon-ing o - ver Moon-light
Can - dle   lights gleaming on the si - lent

Bay,_____   Ban - jos   strum,   tun-ing while the
shore;_____   Lone - ly   nights,   dream-ing till we

78

moon beams play.____ All a - lone,___ un - known
meet once more.____ Far a - part,___ her heart___

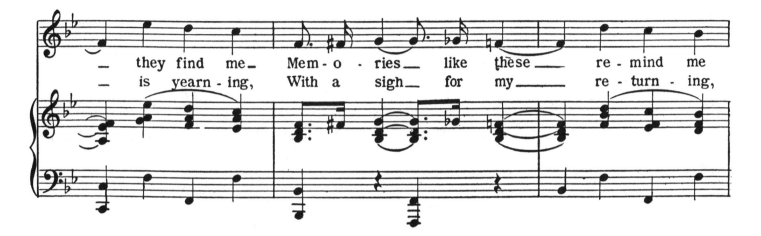

___ they find me___ Mem - o - ries___ like these___ re - mind me
___ is yearn - ing, With a sigh___ for my___ re - turn - ing,

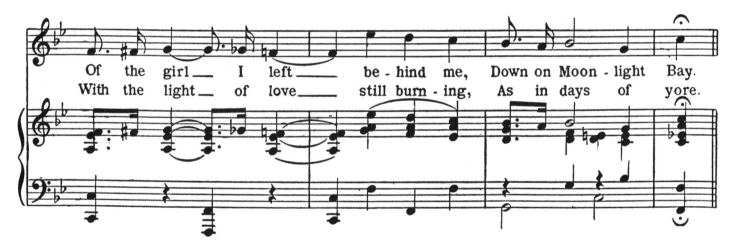

Of the girl___ I left___ be - hind me, Down on Moon - light Bay.
With the light___ of love___ still burn - ing, As in days of yore.

CHORUS

We were sail - ing a - long_____ On Moon - light

p-f

Bay, _____ We could hear the voic-es ring - ing, _____ They seemed to

say _____ "You have stol-en her heart, _____

___ Now don't go 'way!" _____ As we sang Love's Old Sweet

Song, On Moon-light Bay _____ We were sail-ing a - -

My Melancholy Baby.

Words by
GEO. A. NORTON.

Music by
ERNIE BURNETT.

Come sweet-heart mine, Dont sit and pine, Tell me of the cares that make you
Birds in the trees, Whis-per-ing breeze, Should not fail to lul you in to

feel so blue. What have I done? An-swer me, Hon',
peace-ful dreams. So tell me why Sad-ly you sigh,

Have I ev-er said an un-kind word to you? My love is true,
Sit-ting at the win-dow where the pale moon beams, You should-n't grieve,

And just for you, I'd do al-most an-y thing at an-y time,
Try and be - lieve, Life is al-ways sun-shine when the heart beats true;

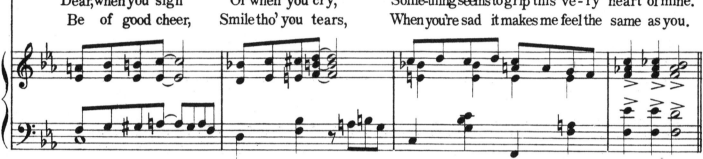

Dear, when you sigh Or when you cry, Some-thing seems to grip this ve-ry heart of mine.
Be of good cheer, Smile tho' you tears, When you're sad it makes me feel the same as you.

Chorus.

Come to me, my mel-an-chol - y ba - by, Cud-dle up and don't be

p-f

blue; All your fears are fool-ish fan-cy, may be,

My Melancholy Baby.

Chorus in march time.

Come to me my mel-an-cho-ly ba - by, Cud-dle up and don't feel blue, ____ All your fears are fool-ish fan-cy may be, You know, dear that I am strong for you, _____ Ev'-ry cloud must have a sil - ver lin - ing, Wait un-til the sun shines through, ____ Smile my hon-ey dear, while I kiss a-way each tear, Or else I shall be mel-an-cho - ly too. ____

My Wife's Gone To The Country

Hurrah! Hurrah!

Sung With
Great Success
By :~

Words & Music By
Geo. Whiting
Irving Berlin
and
Ted Snyder

5

Ted Snyder Co.
Music Publishers
112 West 36 St. New York.

"My Wife's Gone To The Country."

(HURRAH ! HURRAH !)

Words by
GEO. WHITING & IRVING BERLIN.

Music by
TED. SNYDER.

When Mrs............ Brown told
He kept the 'phone a

hub - by, "I just can't stand the heat, Please
go - ing, Told ev' - ry - one he knew, "It's

send me to the coun - try, dear, I know 'twould be a
Mis - ter Brown, come on down town, I have some news for

treat." Next day his wife and fam' - ly were
you." He told a friend — re - port - er — just

seat - ed on a train, And when the train had
why he felt so gay, Next day an ad - ver -

start - ed, Brown - ie shout - ed this re - frain.
tise - ment, in the pa - pers read this way.

My Wife's Gone To The Country.

(Extra verses)

3

He sang his joyful story into a phonograph
He made a dozen records, and I say it was to laugh
For when his friends had vanished, and Brown was all alone,
His neighbors heard the same old tune on Brownies graphophone.
CHORUS
My wife's gone to the country, hurrah, hurrah!
She thought it best, I need the rest, that's why she went away.
She took the children with her, hurrah, hurrah!
Like Eva Tanguay I don't care, my wife's gone away.

4

He went into the parlor and tore down from the wall
A sign that read "God Bless Our Home" and threw it in the hall,
Another sign he painted and hung it up instead.
Next day the servant nearly fainted when these words she read.
CHORUS
My wife's gone to the country, hurrah, hurrah!
She thought it best, I need the rest, that's why she went away.
She took the children with her, hurrah, hurrah!
Now I'm with you, if you're with me, my wife's gone away.

5

He called on pretty Molly, a girl he used to know,
The servant said "She left the house about an hour ago,
But if you leave your name, sir, or write a little note,
I'll give it to her when she comes," and this is what he wrote.
CHORUS
My wife's gone to the country, hurrah, hurrah!
She thought it best, I need the rest, that's why she went away.
She took the children with her, hurrah, hurrah!
I love my wife, but oh! you kid, my wife's gone away.

6

He went and bought a parrot, a very clever bird,
The kind that always would repeat most anything she heard.
So when his voice grew husky, and Brownie couldn't talk
While he'd be taking cough-drops, he would have the parrot squawk
CHORUS
My wife's gone to the country, hurrah, hurrah!
She thought it best, I need the rest, that's why she went away.
She took the children with her, hurrah, hurrah!
I knew my book, she left the cook, my wife's gone away.

THE OLD RUGGED CROSS

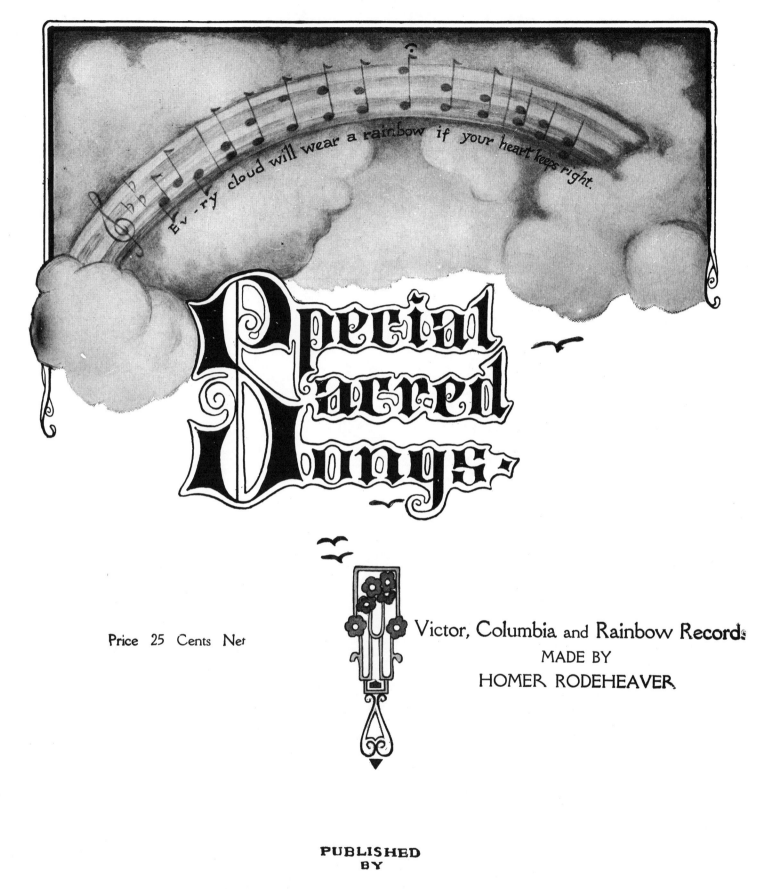

Ev-ry cloud will wear a rainbow if your heart keeps right.

Special Sacred Songs

Price 25 Cents Net

Victor, Columbia and Rainbow Records
MADE BY
HOMER RODEHEAVER

PUBLISHED
BY

THE RODEHEAVER COMPANY,

218 S. Wabash Ave.
CHICAGO.

721 Arch St.
PHILADELPHIA.

THE OLD RUGGED CROSS

G. B.

REV. GEO. BENNARD

1. On a hill far a - way stood an old rug-ged cross, The___
2. Oh, that old rug-ged cross, so de-spied by the world, Has a
3. In the old rug-ged cross, stained with blood so di - vine, A___
4. To the old rug-ged cross I will ev - er be true, Its___

em - blem of suf - f'ring and shame, ___ And I love that old cross where the
won-d'rous at - trac - tion for me, ___ For the dear Lamb of God left His
won - d'rous beau - ty I see; ___ For 'twas on that old cross Je - sus
shame and reproach glad - ly bear; ___ Then He'll call me, some day, to my

THE $1000.00 PRIZE SONG

PEG O'MY HEART

WRITTEN AROUND
J. Hartley Manners
WONDERFUL CHARACTER
"PEG" in Oliver Morosco's
PRODUCTION
of the COMEDY
"PEG O'MY HEART"
at the
CORT THEATRE N.Y.
Dedicated to the Star
MISS LAURETTE TAYLOR

Words by
ALFRED BRYAN
Music by
FRED FISHER

Laurette Taylor

60

LEO. FEIST INC. POPULAR EDITION NEW YORK
ASCHERBERG HOPWOOD & CREW, LTD. LONDON ENGLAND

Peg O' My Heart.

Words by
ALFRED BRYAN

Music by
FRED. FISCHER

Oh! my heart's in a whirl, Ov - er
When your hearts full of fears, And your

one lit - tle girl, I love her, I love her, yes, I
eyes full of tears, I'll kiss them, I'll kiss them all a -

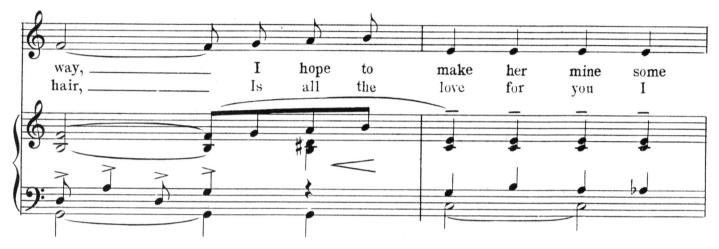

Sweet-er than the rose of Er - in, are your win-ning smiles en-dear-in', Peg O' My Heart,

Your glan - ces with Ir - ish art en - trance us,

Come, be my own,— Come, make your home in my heart.

heart.

Row, Row, Row.

Words by
William Jerome.

Music by
Jimmie V. Monaco.

Young John - nie Jones he had a cute lit - tle boat,____
Right in his boat he had a cute lit - tle seat,____

And all the girl - ies he would take for a float.____
And ev - 'ry kiss he stole from Flo was so sweet.____

af - ter - noon, ___ She'd jump in his boat ___ and they would spoon. ___
tell to Flo, ___ Un - til it was time ___ for them to go. ___

Chorus.

And then he'd row, row, row, Way up the Riv - er he would

row, row, row, A hug he'd give her, Then he'd kiss her now and

then, She would tell him when, He'd fool a-round and fool a-round and

then they'd kiss a - gain, and then he'd row, row, row   a lit - tle

furth - er he would row, oh, oh, oh, oh, _____ 1. Then he'd
2. With her

drop both his oars, ___ Take a few more en - cores __ and then he'd
head on his breast__ Then there's twen - ty bars rest__

row,   row,   row. ____ And then he'd row. ____

SNOOKEY OOKUMS
By
IRVING
BERLIN
BESSIE KAPLAN
WATERSON·BERLIN & SNYDER Co
MUSIC PUBLISHERS
112 WEST 38TH ST. NEW YORK

SNOOKEY OOKUMS

By IRVING BERLIN

I live right next door,_____ In a-part-ment for-ty-
You would bet your life _____ That they were-n't man and

-four._____ Gee! but they're a mush-y He and she,
wife._____ He's a lit-tle fel-low, four foot tall,

Mush-ing seems to be their spec-ial-ty, It would
Weigh-ing just a hun-dred clothes and all; She's a

start you walk-ing, If you heard them talk-ing.
great big la-dy, Weighs a hun-dred eigh-ty.

All night long he calls her Snooky oo-kums, Snooky oo-kums,

All night long the neighbors shout, "Cut it out! cut it out! cut it out!"

They cry, "For good-ness sake! Don't keep us all a-wake,

With your snooky, ook-ey, ook-ey, ba-by talk! talk!

The Sweetheart Of Sigma Chi

Words by
BYRON D. STOKES
Alpha Pi '13

Music by
F. DUDLEIGH VERNOR
Alpha Pi '14

When the world goes wrong as it's
Ev - 'ry mag - ic breeze wafts a

bound to do, And you've brok - en Dan Cu - pid's bow, And you
kiss to you From the lips of your "sweet six - teen," And

long for the girl you used to love The maid of the long a -
one by one the maids you knew Bow to your Meer-schaum

go; Why light your pipe bid sor - row a-vaunt! Blow the
Queen. As the years drift by on the tides of time, And they

rit.

smoke from your al-tar of dreams And wreathe the face of your
all have for-got-ten but you, Then the girl of your dreams the

dream girl there The love that is just what it seems.
sweet - er seems, She's the girl who is al - ways true.

rit.

CHORUS

The girl of my dreams is the sweet-est girl Of all the girls I know. Each
sweet co--ed, like a rain bow trail Fades in the af - ter glow. The
blue of her eyes and the gold of her hair Are a blend of the west-ern sky; And the
moon-light beams on the girl of my dreams She's the Sweet-heart of Sig-ma Chi! _____

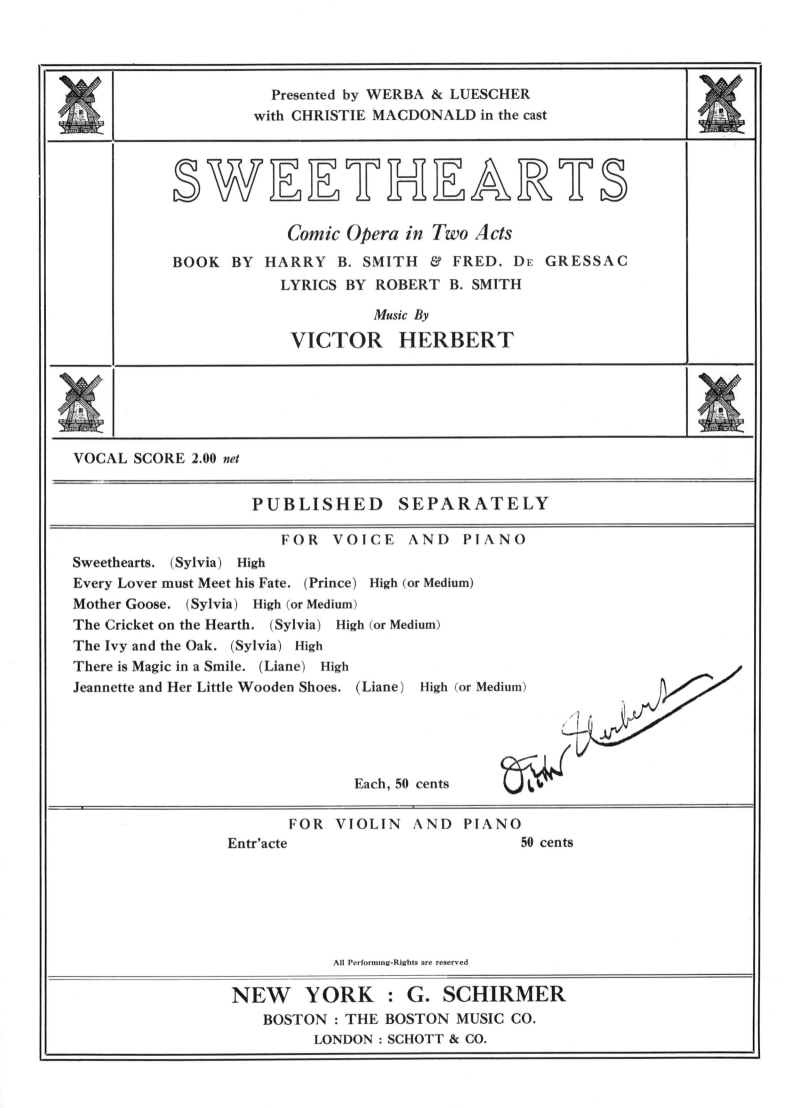

Presented by WERBA & LUESCHER
with CHRISTIE MACDONALD in the cast

SWEETHEARTS

Comic Opera in Two Acts

BOOK BY HARRY B. SMITH & FRED. DE GRESSAC
LYRICS BY ROBERT B. SMITH

Music By

VICTOR HERBERT

VOCAL SCORE 2.00 *net*

PUBLISHED SEPARATELY

FOR VOICE AND PIANO

Sweethearts. (Sylvia) High

Every Lover must Meet his Fate. (Prince) High (or Medium)

Mother Goose. (Sylvia) High (or Medium)

The Cricket on the Hearth. (Sylvia) High (or Medium)

The Ivy and the Oak. (Sylvia) High

There is Magic in a Smile. (Liane) High

Jeannette and Her Little Wooden Shoes. (Liane) High (or Medium)

Each, 50 cents

FOR VIOLIN AND PIANO

Entr'acte   50 cents

NEW YORK : G. SCHIRMER

BOSTON : THE BOSTON MUSIC CO.

LONDON : SCHOTT & CO.

Sweethearts

Lyrics by
Robert B. Smith

From the Comic Opera
"Sweethearts," by
Victor Herbert

114

Sympathy

WALTZ-SONG
From the Comedy-Opera "The Firefly"

Otto Hauerbach

Geraldine and Thurston

Rudolf Friml

Ger. Um - hm! _____ Um - hm! _____ *Thurst.* Dry up those dew - drops and
Thurst. Um - uh! _____ Um - uh! _____ *Ger.* There's not a thing that I

look at me! What you're in need of is sym - pa - thy.
would not do, If on - ly he would be sweet like you.

REFRAIN

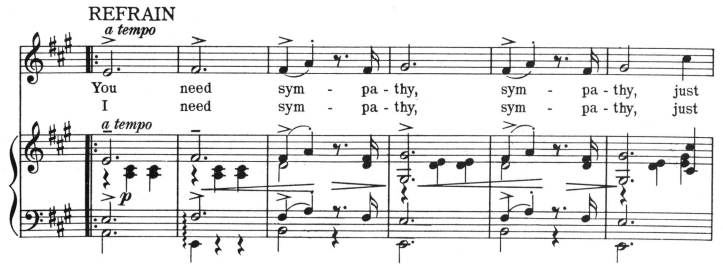

You need sym - pa - thy, sym - pa - thy, just
I need sym - pa - thy, sym - pa - thy, just

sym - pa - thy! You won't think I am free,
sym - pa - thy! I won't think you are free,

You will not scold or say I am bold When I treat
I will not scold nor say you are bold When you treat

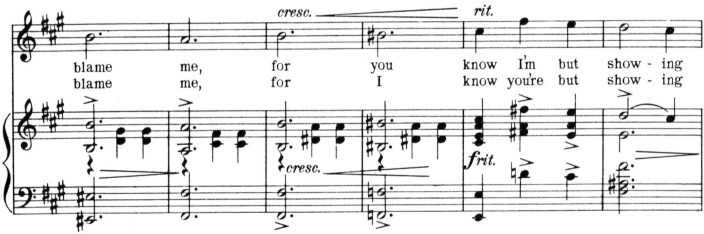

you ten - der - ly, ten - der - ly! Don't
me ten - der - ly, ten - der - ly! Don't

blame me, for you know I'm but show - ing
blame me, for I know you're but show - ing

sym - pa - thy! -thy!
sym - pa - thy! -thy!

REFRAIN

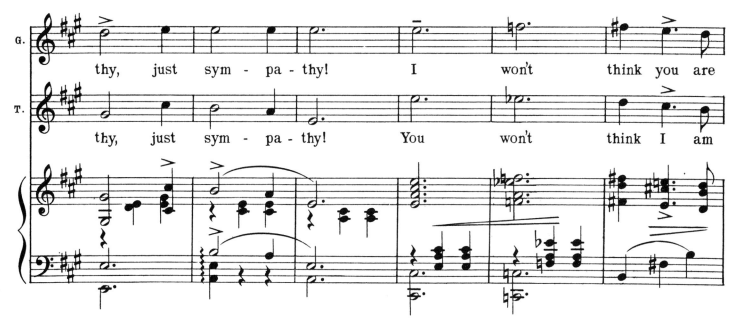

The International Rag

by IRVING BERLIN

You got ex - cit - ed and you start - ed some - thing
Has start - ed eve - ry bo - dy danc - ing dai - ly

na - tions jump - ing all a - round___ You've got a lot to
Pranc - ing gai - ly all a - round___ There's syn - co - pa - tion

an - swer for___ They lay the blame right at your door___
in the air___ They've got the fev - er eve - ry where

The world is rag - time cra - zy from shore to shore___
Each hap - py, snap - py chap - py cries "It's a bear,"___

London dropped it's dig - ni - ty___ So has France and Ger - man - y___

All hands are danc-ing to a rag-ged-y mel-o-dy Full of o-rig-i-nal-i-ty

The folks who live in sun - ny Spain_____ dance to a

strain _____ that they call the Span-ish Tan - - go

Sung by
Mr John McCormack

In F *(c to c)* In G *(d to d)* In Ab *(eb to eb)* In Bb *(f to f)* In C *(g to g)*

Duet in F

Contralto or Baritone *(lead) (c to c)*

Soprano or Tenor *(a to g)*

Duet in C

Soprano or Tenor *(lead) (g to g)*

Contralto or Baritone *(e to d)*

There's A Long, Long Trail

SONG

WRITTEN BY

STODDARD KING

COMPOSED BY

ZO ELLIOTT

Solo 60 Cents   Duet 75 Cents
Octavo, Male, Female and Mixed Voices **15** cents

THE WITMARK BLACK AND WHITE SERIES

M. Witmark & Sons,

NEW YORK • CHICAGO • LONDON.

There's A Long, Long Trail

Written by
STODDARD KING

Composed by
ZO ELLIOTT

Nights are grow-ing ver - y lone - ly, Days are ver - y
All night long I hear you call - ing, Call - ing sweet and

long;⸺ I'm a - grow-ing wear - y on - ly
low;⸺ Seem to hear your foot-steps fall - ing,

List - 'ning for your song._____ Old re - mem - bran - ces are
Ev - 'ry where I go._____ Tho' the road be - tween us

throng - ing Thro' my mem - o - ry.____ Till it seems the world is
stretch - es Man - y a wear - y mile.____ I for - get that you're not

full of dreams Just to call you back to me.____
with me yet, When I think I see you smile.____

CHORUS *Evenly with much expression*

There's a long, long trail a - wind - ing In to the land of my

p — f a tempo

dreams,__ Where the night - in-gales are sing - ing And a white moon

beams:____ There's a long, long night of wait - ing___ Un - til my

dreams all come true;____ Till the day when I'll be

go - ing down That long, long trail with you. There's a you.____

Marching Chorus Published by Popular Request

In Martial Time *(But not fast)*

There's a long, long trail a wind-ing____ In-to the land of____ my dreams,____ ____ Where the night - in - gales are sing - ing And a white moon beams:____ There's a long, long night of wait - ing____ Un-til my dreams all____ ____ come true;____ Till the day when I'll be go - ing down That long, long trail with you. There's a you.

The Trail Of The Lonesome Pine

Words by
BALLARD MACDONALD

Music by
HARRY CARROLL

134

girl of mine. Her name is June, and ver - y, ver - y soon,
rap - ture trills; They seem to say "Your June is lone - some too,"

She'll be - long to me, For I know she's
Long - ing fills her eyes, She is wait - ing

wait - ing there for me, 'Neath that lone pine tree.
for you pa - tient - ly, Where the pine tree sighs.

rall.

REFRAIN

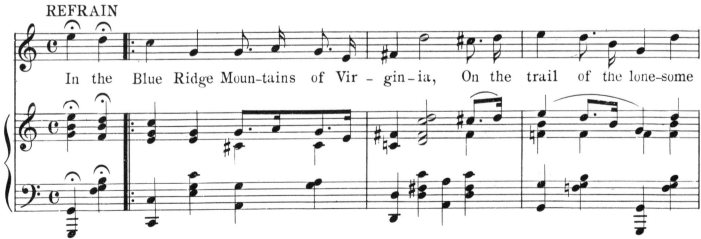

In the Blue Ridge Moun - tains of Vir - gin - ia, On the trail of the lone - some

pine _____ In the pale moon-shine our hearts entwine, Where she carved her name and

I carved mine; Oh, June, _____ like the moun-tains I'm blue _ Like the

pine _____ I am lone-some for you, In the Blue Ridge Moun-tains of Vir-

gin - ia, On the trail of the lone-some pine. _____ In the pine.

"Waiting For The Robert E Lee"

Words by
L. WOLFE GILBERT

Music by
LEWIS F. MUIR

Copyright 1912 by F. A. Mills, 122 West 36th St., New York
International Copyright Secured

-ee-- and   Join that shuff - lin'   throng,_____

Hear that   mu - sic   and   song._____   It's sim - ply   great,

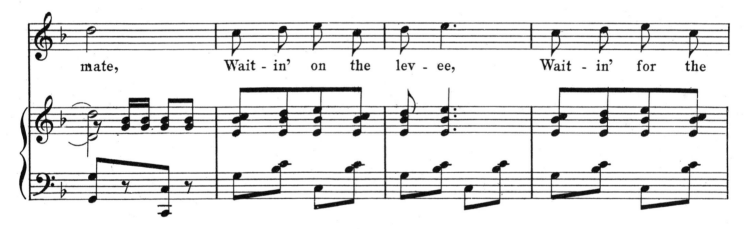

mate,   Wait - in'   on the   lev - ee,   Wait - in'   for the

Rob - ert   E.   Lee._____   Lee._____

D.S.

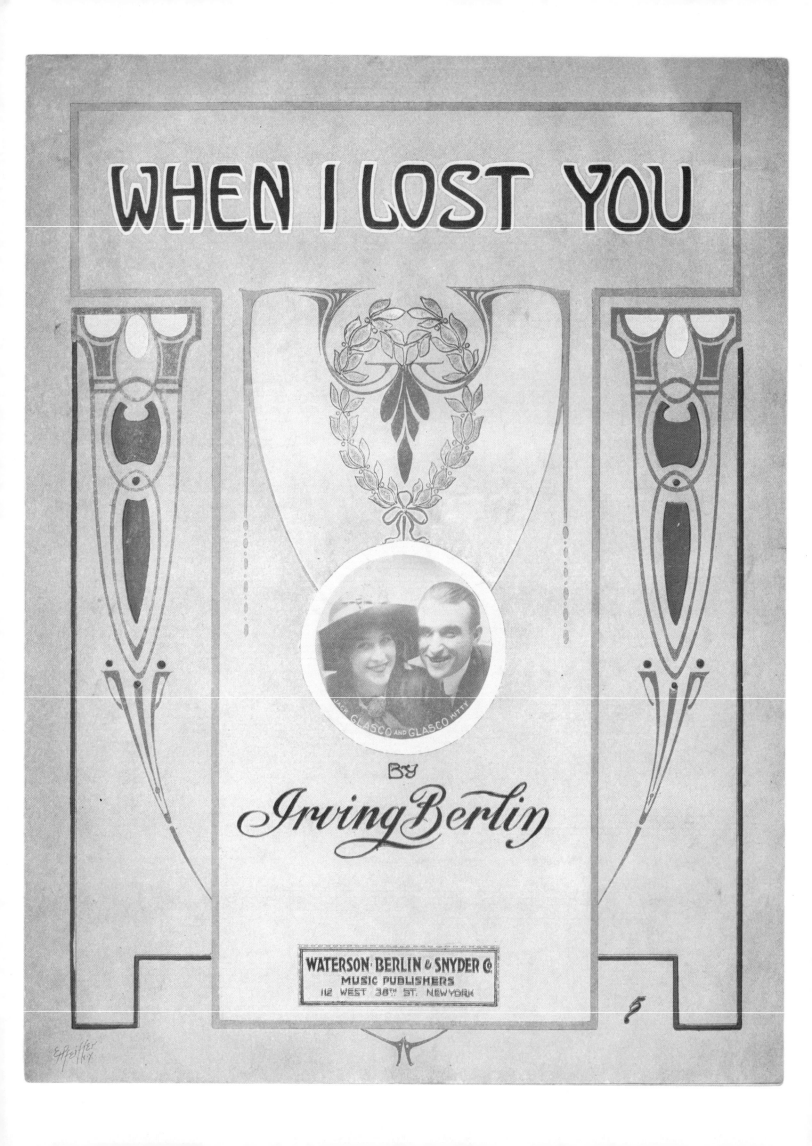

WHEN I LOST YOU

By IRVING BERLIN

I lost the an - gel who gave me Sum - mer, the

whole win - ter through,..................... I lost the glad - ness that

turned in - to sad - ness, When I lost you.......................

When Irish Eyes are Smiling

Chauncey Olcott's

Song Successes

in his
New Production

THE
ISLE O'DREAMS

By RIDA JOHNSON YOUNG
DIRECTION OF MR. HENRY MILLER

M. WITMARK & SONS
NEW YORK · CHICAGO · SAN FRANCISCO · LONDON · PARIS · MELBOURNE

When Irish Eyes Are Smiling

Lyric by
CHAUNCEY OLCOTT
& GEO. GRAFF Jr.

Music by
ERNEST R. BALL

Valse moderato espressive

There's a tear in your eye, And I'm won-der-ing why, For it
For your smile is a part, Of the love in your heart, And it

nev-er should be there at all. _____ With such pow'r in, your smile, Sure a
makes e-ven sun-shine more bright. _____ Like the lin-nets sweet song, Croon-ing

stone you'd be-guile, So there's nev-er a tear-drop should fall. _____ When your
all the day long, Comes your laugh-ter so ten-der and light. _____ For the

sweet lilt - ing laugh - ter's like some fair - y song, And your eyes twink - le
spring-time of life is the sweet-est of all, There is ne'er a real

bright as can be; _____ You should laugh all the while and all
care or re - gret; _____ And while spring-time is ours through-out

oth - er times, while, And now smile a smile for me. _____
all of youth's hours, Let us smile each chance we get. _____

CHORUS

When I - rish eyes are smi - ling, ____ Sure it's like a morn in

NORA BAYES

SONG SUCCESS

WHEN IT'S APPLE BLOSSOM TIME IN NORMANDIE

Written & Composed by
Mellor Gifford & Trevor.

JEROME H. REMICK & CO.

NEW YORK   DETROIT

When It's Apple Blossom Time In Normandy.

With a most per - sua - sive lay, _____ Tho' she was griev - ing,
I shall wish that you will stay." _____ Said he de - spair - ing,
Hap - pi - ness is theirs to - day, _____ 'Mid blos - soms fall - ing,

when he was leav - ing, He con - sol'd her in this way.
"Love, I'm de - clar - ing, I'm in earn - est, when I say.
he is re - call - ing, What he fond - ly used to say.

un poço rall.

Chorus.

"When it's ap - ple blos - som time in Nor - man - dy! I

p - f

want to be in Nor - man - dy, By that dear old

wish ing well, With you, Ma - rie! When it's

ap - ple blos-som time in Nor-man-dy, I'm com-ing back to

woo, And the spring will bring a wed-ding ring, Lit - tle

sweet - heart, to you!" When it's you!"

WHEN THE MIDNIGHT CHOO–CHOO
LEAVES FOR ALABAM'.

By IRVING BERLIN

up my dreary flat,............ Where many wea-ry nights I sat, Think-ing
kiss my Pa and Ma............ A doz-en times for ev'-ry star, Shin-ing

of the folks down home who think of me;............................ You can
o-ver Al-a-ba-ma's new mown hay;............................ I'll be

bet you'll find me sing-ing hap-pi-ly.............................
glad e-nough to throw my-self a-way.............................

CHORUS

When the mid-night choo-choo leaves for Al-a-bam',............................

You Can't Stop Me From Loving You

Lyric by
GERBER and MURPHY

Music by
HENRY I. MARSHALL

Andante

PIANO

VOICE

Sweet - heart, you have asked me if I love you,
When your gold - en hair is turn - ing gray, dear,

With a love that al - ways will be true,
And your eyes have lost their won - drous hue;

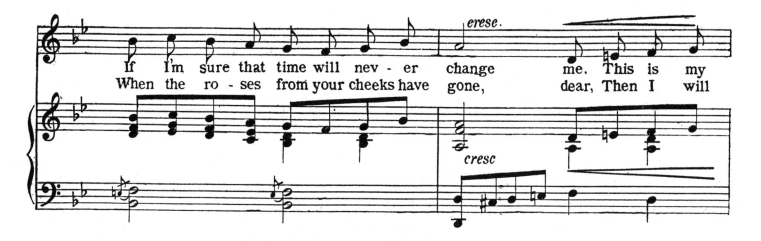

If I'm sure that time will nev - er change me, This is my
When the ro - ses from your cheeks have gone, dear, Then I will

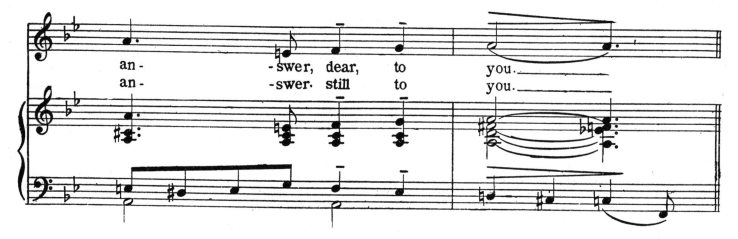

an - -swer, dear, to you.
an - -swer still to you.

REFRAIN
Moderato

You can't stop the winds from blow - ing, You

can't stop the sun's bright light, You can't stop the trees from

grow - ing, You can't stop the moon at night; You

can't stop the birds from fly - ing ___ You can't stop the morn-ing ___

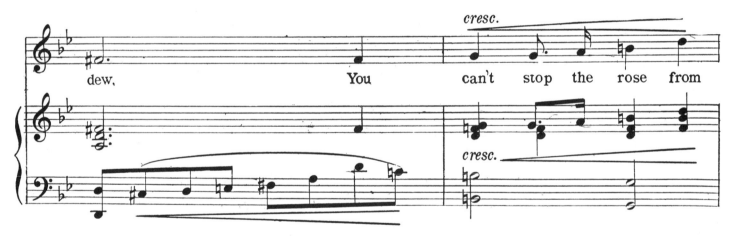

dew, You can't stop the rose from

cresc.

dy - -ing And you can't stop me from lov-ing you. ___

f rit. *mp* *dim.* *pp*

"You Made Me Love You"

(I Did'nt Want To Do It)

Words by
JOE McCARTHY

Music by
JAMES V. MONACO

Your love makes me speak this way,— Why, oh! why should
But I nev-er thought of you,— Now my dream of

I feel blue,— Once I used to laugh at you,— But now I'm
love is o'er,— I want you and noth-ing more,— Come on, en-

cry-ing,— No use de - ny - ing,— There's no one else but you will do,—
fold me,— Come on and hold me— Just like you nev-er did be - fore,—

CHORUS

You made me love you, I did-n't want to do it, I did-n't want to do it,

p-f

You made me want you,   And all the time you knew it   I guess you al-ways knew it,

You made me hap-py some-times   You made me glad ___

But there were times dear, You made me feel _ so bad. ___

You made me sigh for   I did-n't want to tell you   I

did-n't want to tell you   I want some love that's   true, Yes I do, Deed I

do, You know I do.   Give me give   me what I cry for,   You

know you got the brand of kiss-es   that I'd   die   for   You know you

made me love   you._____   you._____